CRUMBS ON THE CARPET

Scarborough and the Legacy of Wilfred Owen's Final Year 1917 - 1918

S F TAYLOR

About the Author

SF Taylor was born in Kingston Upon Hull but has also lived in Bradford, Birmingham, Aberdeen and Toronto. She has had several short stories published including a competition winning title, *The Package.* She has also written *This Squalid Little Room* incorporating Lawrence of Arabia's stays in Hornsea shortly before his death. She currently lives in Hornsea, East Yorkshire.

For further details on SF Taylor visit SF Taylor Author

facebook.com/sftaylorauthor

twitter.com/SueFraserTaylo1

instagram.com/soofraser

Also By S.F.Taylor

This Squalid Little Room (T.E.Lawrence in Hornsea, East Yorkshire)
The Plotting Shed (Two short stories)
A Quick Read (Short story)

Published 2020

ISBN: 978-1-8382517-2-7

Thank you to Thom Strid for yet another brilliant cover design.

Thanks also to Amanda Allen of The Coffeehouse Writer for her
continued support and guidance.

*"War is not a life: it is a situation,
one which may neither be ignored
nor accepted"*

T.S. Eliot

*Dedicated to the families of
fallen soldiers in all wars*

Contents

Introduction

2018 brought to a close four years of centenary commemorations of the First World War. Since 1918, there have been many changes in attitude to war and conflict: the concepts of how and why; what if; and the ubiquitous 'lessons to be learned'. They have changed as consecutive generations proselytise their own particular truth.

Museums, villages, towns and cities have exposed their histories to help following generations understand what happened and to reflect upon the aftermath of war. The debate will not stop, nor should it when there is inevitable loss of life bringing devastation to the countries involved and the people left behind.

The concept of chivalrous, righteous combat, still prevalent at the start of the First World War, was blown apart once the reality was laid open for scrutiny. Scarborough was re-assessing its attitude as early as 1914 following an attack on the town by the German navy when innocent civilians, including a baby, were killed. Over the centuries, this small seaside town had developed and grown, utilising its natural resources of spa waters and the North Sea, or

German Ocean as it was once named. At the turn of the century, life was good; the newly established railway brought in increasing numbers of visitors and the lure of the seaside was on the increase for less fortunate, land-locked, inhabitants of industrial towns. By the time Wilfred Owen arrived, the mood of the town was not so joyous, however.

Owen enlisted shortly before conscription would have forced him into joining. He took reference at the time from the celebrated French poet, Tailhade, believing that language would be the major casualty. They were both poorly informed and it showed. The French and British public were deliberately kept in ignorance of what was really happening. For Owen, loss of the English language was a sufficient and righteous reason to fight.

As war played out across Europe, Owen inevitably dismissed his earlier preconceptions. The issue of language was not brought up again and he even took pains to continue to learn German. He would also scorn the 'old lie' of Horace, when he wrote the memorable 'Dulce et decorum est/Pro patria mori' (It is sweet and fitting to die for one's country). The reality of combat and dying for one's country left little room for chivalry and honour.

This book reflects upon how the War changed Owen's life; the effect it had upon his writing and his beliefs; his relationships with those around him; and of course the legacy he leaves behind. The time he spent in Scarborough would sadly be the last months of his life, but it was also a time when he wrote and refined his finest work, revealing much about the man as well as the poet and the soldier. He also leaves numerous letters, mostly written to his mother. He began writing to her from the tender age of five, very regularly, until just days before his death twenty years later.

The atrocities Owen witnessed transformed his writing,

turning him into one of the most insightful and highly respected poets of the First World War. He showed great empathy for the men serving under him and his poetry spoke out against the ignorance of a society that failed to understand the brutality, the misery and the suffering.

Soldiers had been castigated as cowards when they presented symptoms of what we now know as 'shell shock', no matter how bravely they had fought, and there was a time when Owen himself was viewed under that particular misapprehension.

From 1915 onwards, when Owen enlisted in the Artists' Rifles, his life irrevocably changed, and in 1918 it was tragically shortened. Scarborough would be the calm before the storm; a time of recuperation and reflection; and a time for planning a future. Sadly for Owen, it was also the beginning of the end. His legacy lives on though and will continue to do so by virtue of the many questions he raised about the morality, and the reality, of that brutal conflict.

SF Taylor
Southfield Writers
August 2020

Scarborough, good for your health

From the seventeenth century onwards, Scarborough continued to thrive. It had begun to fully optimise its mineral waters, a natural resource that became highly valuable to the town. Increasing numbers of people across the country were certain that the waters were a cure for all manner of ailments. During the 1660s, the nobility sought its medicinal qualities and readily imbibed the foul tasting liquid in the belief that it was acting as a cure for a variety of ailments from gout to arthritis.

By the late 18th century, bathing in seawater was also promoted as beneficial for health and well being, although the fun part of relaxing on a beach in the sun, as well as sea bathing, would soon follow.

Owen once described Scarborough as a town where 'there's not a house built since 1780, not a street much wider than Claus and miles of it, mind you, miles of glorious eighteenth century.' [Emile Claus: the rotund Belgian painter befriended by Owen]

Anne Bronte stayed in Scarborough in 1848, during what would be the final weeks of her life after she had persuaded her sister Charlotte that the Scarborough air and waters would be good for her health. Anne had previously spent time at this beautiful seaside town as a governess and it had proved more than fruitful in her writing. She spent several years exploring the length and breadth of the Scarborough landscape and it provided her with a vivid backdrop to draw on as she soaked up the dramatic cliffs and wild seas, the stunning walkways and the beautiful architecture.

Sketch of Anne Bronte by her sister Charlotte

Anne had always felt a close affinity with Scarborough, but sadly, her condition (consumption) had deteriorated too far. After a few short weeks, on 28 May 1849, she died and was buried shortly after at St. Mary's Church, beneath the ruins of the castle on the cliff top. It is very likely that Owen would have visited at some point during his stay.

During the late nineteenth century, great music hall stars flocked to the Spa Theatre, enhancing and capitalising on the success of the seaside holiday. The town blossomed, making the most of what it had to offer and by the mid nineteenth century, Scarborough, along with its neighbouring towns of Bridlington, Filey and Hornsea, brought in swathes of new visitors via a rapidly expanding railway network. Holidaymakers flocked in, keen to escape the grime and monotony of working life in the inner towns and cities. The trend towards cheap accommodation and accessible travel burgeoned and the beaches filled to capacity during the summer months.

Other developments soon followed: Marine Drive opened in 1908, linking the two bays; the oriental themed Peasholm Park opened in 1912; and electric trams ran through the streets. Scarborough in the 1900s was a spa town that attracted increasing numbers of visitors and holidaymakers.

Scarborough Railway Poster 1930

As the First World War approached, this thriving Scarborough and its inhabitants were ill prepared for the devastation of the next stage in its history.

Scarborough at war

On Wednesday 16th December 1914, under cover of darkness, the First World War arrived on Scarborough's doorstep as six German battle cruisers made their way through the minefields of the North Sea. They were targeting Scarborough, Whitby and Hartlepool on the Eastern coastline. Within minutes, the people of those towns understood what the reality of war with Germany would mean to them on personal level and not just something that was happening on the battlefields of the Western Front. The shock of that morning could not have been greater.

The attack lasted thirty minutes during which schools, shops, churches and homes were laid to rubble in a raid that was intended to show the might of a resurgent German Navy.

Amongst the public properties hit were Scarborough Castle, the Grand Hotel where Anne and Charlotte Bronte had stayed, and three churches. The attacks on all three towns resulted in the deaths of 137 people and the casualty toll reached 592, most of whom were civilians.

The bomb-damaged Grand Hotel, Scarborough
1914 (Topham Picturepoint/Press Association)

This meticulously planned raid had an enormous effect on the British public, bringing outrage towards Germany for attacking civilians, and anger against the Royal Navy for its inability to prevent it.

The outrage perpetrated by Germany became part of a UK wide propaganda campaign, creating a huge surge of patriotism and recruitment following this abhorrent loss of civilian life.

Posters appealed to the men of Britain to do
their duty and enlist. 1915. (Imperial War
Museum)

The words 'Remember Scarborough' were used on recruitment posters to great effect after civilians had proved an easy target for the German Navy, and Winston Churchill branded the Germans 'baby killers' when 14-month-old John Shields Ryall became known as the youngest killed during the attack. First Lord of the Admiralty, Winston Churchill wrote to the Mayor of Scarborough, Mr. C.C. Graham:

'Dear Mr Mayor

I send you a message of sympathy not only on my own account but on behalf of the Navy, in the losses Scarborough has sustained. We mourn with you the peaceful inhabitants who have been killed or maimed,

and particularly the women and children. We admire the dignity and fortitude with which Scarborough, Whitby and Hartlepool have confronted outrage. We share your disappointment that the miscreants escaped unpunished. We await with patience the opportunity that will surely come.'

The full letter and reply by the Mayor are kept for posterity at the Scarborough Maritime Heritage Centre in the town.

One of the most iconic posters following the 1914 attack on Scarborough, was this successful and emotive encouragement of recruitment to the British forces (Library of Congress)

The German attack was perceived as a 'crime' and not just an outcome of war (Poster origin unknown)

The shocking attack on the town, so shortly following the onset of war, dramatically shaped the British perception of Germany and the mood of the people across the nation radically changed. It was clearly a wake up call that Germany meant business and that they were willing to go to unprecedented lengths to achieve their goal in the domination of Britain and Europe. This was a war that made great use of innovative and devastating technology, of machine guns, poison gas and flame-throwers. The era of chivalry was long gone and the expectations of young men like Owen, that the war would be a justified and glorious campaign of right overcoming might, were soon laid waste in the bloody, muddy battle fields of France.

The Mayor of Scarborough understood this in his reference to German sailors who were disregarding the 'glorious old traditions of the sea'.

Owen had also come to learn that war bore no reference to any mythical notion of chivalry and honour in a poetic sense. By the time he arrived in Scarborough in 1917, he had acquired a much greater understanding, both on a personal and a global level. Prior to his experience at the Front, life had presented little cause for any serious concerns but he, like many others of his generation, was pulled up short by the brutality they would endure.

A further notable attack had taken place in Scarborough on September 4 1917, just two months before Owen's arrival. On a fine summer's evening, a German submarine surfaced in Cayton Bay and prepared to fire on the minesweeping fleet stationed there (the fleet consisted of boats that were basically no more than armed trawlers crewed by fishermen). This later attack, however, brought few casualties and the submarine disappeared upon retaliation. Although there were three fatalities upon shore, despite the target being at sea, the incident did not raise anywhere near the same outrage as the attack of 1914, possibly due to the fact that the target was actually at sea.

3

Owen's family life and early years

Wilfred Edward Salter was born in 1893 at Oswestry, Shropshire, close to the Welsh border, to Susan and Tom Owen. Susan's parents believed that their daughter had married beneath her when Tom was no more than a railway clerk, but he worked his way up to station master and proved to be a solid and reliable husband and father. There were four children from the marriage: Wilfred, Mary, Colin and Harold, of whom Wilfred was the eldest. The family was close knit and although they struggled financially for a time, with a drop in circumstances, they did not suffer too much from it. The children grew up with cousins close by and maintained contact with them as they grew older. As the first born, Wilfred held an inordinately special place in his mother's heart, a point often remarked upon after his death and one that undoubtedly came to have a bearing upon his nature as well as his social standing. However, his life up to the start of the War had had little cause for concern.

Owen's early years were shrouded by an evangelical

doctrine, which had much to do with his mother, but religion did not play too great a role in his life. Their family was not alone in embracing evangelism, but Owen's views on religion would radically alter in his later years, and more especially when the violence and brutality of the War kicked in.

Despite the drop in status when the family had to leave Plas Wilmot (the beloved ancestral home of Susan's parents) the family nevertheless enjoyed holidays together and at least one was spent at Scarborough, at the home of Susan's cousin, May Susan Davies. Cousin May ran a girls' school at Pavilion Square and their boys played cricket on North Bay beach, as Owen would recall in later years when he was stationed in the town. Pavilion Square was built and developed during the late 19th century, and undoubtedly enhanced the town with its presence.

Pavilion Square started life with plush homes overlooking tennis courts and a bowling green and was surrounded by trees. By 1870, the Square also boasted the magnificent Pavilion Hotel.

Owen spent Christmas Eve, 1917 with Cousin May at Pavilion Square where they were joined by another lady, Miss Bennett. She offered him German lessons and Owen appears to have taken her up on it, keen to continue to learn the language. He had started in France, at the Berlitz School in Bordeaux, where he had taught for a while. This was despite the earlier fears that his own language might be compromised should Germany win the war.

'I went to tea with Cousin May again, & had a German lesson from a lady staying there!

Would you please send me (1) Berlitz German Book...'

Letter to Susan Owen, 27 December 1917

Pavillion Square and Hotel, Scarborough (Max Payne Collection)

Susan Owen, devoted mother

Wilfred was always a prolific letter writer, especially to his mother, and of the 554 of his letters to survive, almost all were written directly to her (others include just one to Susan and his father together and four to Tom alone). His letters began from the age of 5 and the earliest known was discovered in Susan's jewellery box in an envelope marked 'Wilfie's first letter, 1898'. They would continue very regularly until 4 days before his death, 20 years later, in 1918.

Young Wilfred in a soldier's uniform made by his
mother (Imperial War Museum)

Owen's devotion to his mother is evident in those
letters as well as in his poetry. He continued to show his
unabated love and affection, from childhood to adoles-
cence, and on into his adult years. At the Front, on 4
February 1917, under extreme conditions of freezing cold
and the constant expectation of attack, he writes:

'The intensity of your Love reached me and kept me
living. I thought of you and Mary without a break all the
time...We were all half-crazed by the buffeting of the
High Explosives...We were marooned on a frozen
desert.'

Her influence on his life can also be witnessed in a
display of constant mindfulness of her situation. Susan
suffered with ill health during much of her adult life, and
perhaps, as it has been suggested, not a little hypochondria

too. Wilfred, ever solicitous of her health and well being, encouraged her in recovery after these bouts of illness, suggesting she should get out more and exercise, encouraging her to take the occasional glass of claret even though she deplored alcohol.

The closeness of mother and son has generated a great debate on Owen's inability to forge a relationship with other females, or indeed anyone, outside of the total and all consuming commitment she showed to him. Owen himself acknowledged as much and at times positively luxuriated in her all-consuming love.

The debate around Owen's sexuality almost certainly leads to the belief that he was in fact homosexual. Had he lived, and had the War not focused so much of his attention, perhaps this would have become more obvious in later life. His poetry and his experiences of war are the overriding factors of Owen's short life and considering the many personal letters and papers that were subsequently destroyed by Susan and by his cousin Leslie Gunston after his death, there is little actual evidence of his sexual inclinations. It became almost an irrelevance.

Susan Owen

If it appears that Susan was not aware of her son's leanings towards the male sex, other than through poetry and friendship; it was suppressed and/or hidden. Homosexuality could not be contemplated in the context of her religion, let alone its illegality during his lifetime. Indeed, she was even appalled at the attention he received from the women he encountered. When he told her of the interest the Leger ladies in France were showing him (both mother and daughter) she also worried about the effect that they were having on her son. Wilfred allayed those fears and made it clear to his mother as well as Mme. Leger that he simply was not interested.

Despite this kind of attention, however, Owen was never put off staying with the family, especially when the benefits to his social standing; the welcome introductions; and the opportunity to develop his poetry, outweighed anything else. He rather basked in it and the years in France would appear to be amongst his happiest.

Tom Owen, a father left behind

The relationship between Tom and Wilfred was by no means as close as the one with his mother, but it was not one of estrangement either. Curiously, in a letter to Sassoon in 1917, Owen wrote:

'I can't get sociable with my father without going back on myself over ten years of thought.'

There is little to establish that Tom was not close to Wilfred given the chance, indeed when they were thrown together there was a suggestion of affection and consideration. It was Tom who first took his eldest son to Brittany in France in 1908 (and again in 1909) to improve his French, and the reports of both trips were very favourable. Owen's mother often had periods of absence from the family home, due to her ill health, and this gave his father at least a chance of developing a relationship with his son, something that seemed to be denied when she was present, such was her closeness to her son.

Tom ensured that his sons attended the best schools possible, both at Birkenhead and Shrewsbury; he understood the benefits of a good education. He also encouraged all his children to read, providing stirring literature in the home such as the works of Walter Scott and Stevenson's 'Treasure Island' to expand their minds and develop their imagination.

Perhaps as Owen reached his teenage years and turned more and more to books and poetry, as opposed to the more 'manly' pursuits very much urged by his father – exercise, sport and the outdoor life – that Wilfred felt an estrangement.

During 1907, Tom moved the family to Shrewsbury from Birkenhead when he was offered a promotion on the Joint Railways. It was a time of upheaval for all of them, and relationships were probably strained for a while. Money was still tight but at fifteen years of age, Owen sought, and was taken on, as a pupil-teacher, for which he would also have received a small salary for the privilege. He may have had to give up Latin, a great disappointment, but greater prominence was given to biology, botany and geology, which pleased Owen.

Tom Owen, 1914 (Wilfred Owen Association)

Leslie Gunston, cousin, playmate and poet

Owen had a close relationship with his cousin from childhood onwards. They had often played together and Owen spent holidays with the family as a child. In later years, they kept in touch and wrote to one another, connecting more over poetry, rather than the War, as time went on.

Leslie Gunston showed a great interest in literature, and wrote poetry too although little is made of this. As fledgling poets they competed with each other and during the autumn and winter of 1916, Owen, Gunston and another friend played a literary game where all three chose a topic and wrote verses on it for each other to read.

Owen maintained contact with his cousin throughout the War years and from Scarborough, in 1917, he opened up to Gunston of his need to finish the poetry he'd already begun:

> 'I have had some good inspirations in Scarboro', but my need is to revise now, rather than keep piling up 'first drafts'.

Owen told Gunston of his appreciation of the acknowledgements received from Robert Graves and

Siegfried Sassoon, both of whom realised the huge potential of his poetry:

> 'They believe in me these Georgians and I suffer a temptation to be satisfied that they read me; and to remain a poet's poet!'
>
> *12 December, 1917*

Gunston continued writing, even publishing some of his works in a book entitled: 'The Nymph and Other Poems'. It was dedicated 'To Wilfred with affection' and sent to his cousin in Scarborough for approval. Owen, however, appeared to be not much impressed.

4

Early poetic influences

William Wordsworth

In 1908, when Owen was fifteen and living in Birkenhead, he discovered Wordsworth and fell in love with poetry. He was inspired, and in the struggle to find his own voice, absorbed himself in nature and the environment as much as the poets he had read. Even during the latter years of writing, he never forgot, or failed to embrace, his appreciation of the natural world, and the imagery continued to weave its way amongst his words:

> Move him into the sun –
> Gently its touch awoke him once,
> At home, whispering of fields half-sown.
> Always it woke him, even in France,
> Until this morning and this snow.
> If anything might rouse him now
> The kind old sun will know.'
> *Extract, 'Futility', May 1918*

William Wordsworth, 1770-1850

John Ruskin was a proponent of the practical study of nature in education and his writings enhanced Owen's interest in plants, rocks and fossils. It was a rare moment of relief whilst working as an assistant at Dunsden Owen discovered that Wigan, the vicar, was not completely lost to literature; he had heard Ruskin lecture, met the Pre-Raphaelite artist Holman Hunt and may even have been distantly related to William Morris. Whilst still at Dunsden, on a convention visit to the Lake District, Owen cycled a forty-mile round trip to visit Ruskin's house, absenting himself from yet another tedious sermon by a visiting preacher. He met Ruskin's biographer, W.G. Collingwood and enjoyed a delightful afternoon in his company before cycling back to the camp.

Given Owen's continued interest in geology and archaeology, it is more than likely that he would have visited the Rotunda Museum whilst stationed in Scarborough. This unique circular building of 1829 is one of the first to be purpose-built; constructed to a design suggested by William Smith, father of English geology.

John Keats

It is well documented that Keats held a great sway over Owen, from his teenage years onwards when he absorbed himself in the poetry of the Romantic genre. He once even described himself as 'in love' with Keats. The poet was a constant influence and even in Owen's later poetry there remain traces of this early love. Keats would never be forgotten. After reading an account of his life, Owen was so moved he wrote to his mother:

> 'I sometimes feel in reading such books that I would give ten years of life to have been born a hundred years earlier.'

In Teignmouth, 1911, Owen visited the house where Keats had stayed and he knew that he had to see Wentworth Place in London where Keats had penned 'Ode to a Nightingale'. The poet had lived there from 1818, seventeen months before travelling to Italy where he died. It is sad to think that both Keats and Owen did not live beyond 25 years of age, the former due to tuberculosis, the latter from a bullet in the Great War, almost one hundred years apart. The opening words to 'Exposure' echo those of Keats, albeit the subject is far removed:'Our brains ache, in the merciless iced east winds that knive us...

> *Wearied we keep awake because the night is silent...'*
>
> *Extract, Exposure, Wilfred Owen, begun Scarborough, 1917*

> *'My heart aches, and a drowsy numbness pains*

My sense…'

Extract, 'Ode to a Nightingale', John Keats, 1819

'Exposure' relates the time of waiting at the Front, where Owen and his men experienced bitter winter weather and insufficient shelter from the cold.

John Keats 1795-1821 (William Hilton, National Portrait Gallery)

During September 1911, Owen visited the British Museum to look at the original manuscripts of Keats' work, and during the summer of 1912, he wrote 'On Seeing a Lock of Keats's Hair'; his hero-worship showing no sign of abatement.

Had Owen's life continued without the all consuming curse of war, his poetry would have taken on a far different voice and in all probability it would not had the same resonance. His poems may be few in number, but the impact they have had in reference to the War is beyond outstanding.

The New Georgian Poets

1911 was a significant year for Owen: by mid-July he had finished working as a teacher-pupil. Having no specific vocation for anything, floundering as to what his next move would be, he became parish assistant at Dunsden for the Reverend Herbert Wigan, the vicar. A career in the Church had been considered at one time and was actively encouraged by Susan, but in reality, Owen knew that he did not have 'the calling' for such a life. Taking up residence at Dunston vicarage was on the understanding that he would be allowed time to devote himself to his poetry, the one part of his life that he was certain of.

It was at Dunsden that he discovered a new style of poetry, one newly adopted by established writers including John Masefield, Rupert Brooke and Harold Monro.

Monro, like Owen, began writing poetry emulating Keats. He then expanded his vision of the world to promote sexual freedom and reject religion. He became excited at the thought of a future that moved away from the 'Romantic Movement'.

Poets such as Munro stimulated Owen's mind as he struggled in the stifling setting of the vicarage where conversation and poetry were not high on the agenda. The evening silences were agony for Owen when he had no-one to converse with, or confide in. Wigan lacked the most basic skills in that respect. Owen's unhappiness grew daily, but it was at Dunsden where he made his first attempts to break away from the Romantic Movement, embracing an overwhelming desire to develop a new style of poetry.

Harold Monro 1879-1932

Despite the drawbacks of life at Dunsden, Owen continued to dwell in the delights of Keats and it is almost certain that poetry had replaced the prominence of religion in his life. Discovering this new poetry, collectively known as 'Georgian', Owen was hungry and curious to know more. He too wanted to get involved in a movement that proclaimed itself to be shifting away from 'Romanticism'.

The name "Georgian" was given to suggest the start of a new age of poetry, coinciding with the accession of George V in 1910. Rupert Brooke, Siegfried Sassoon, Walter de la Mare, A.E. Housman and D.H. Lawrence were amongst the contributors to the collective; they wanted to make their new poetry accessible to a much wider audience, and with this in mind, a series of anthologies were published. Five volumes of Georgian Poetry, edited by Edward Marsh, were made available between 1912 and 1922.

However, Georgian poetry did not make its mark as

much as they would have liked, or anticipated. Taking inspiration from nature, art and the countryside, much of the poetry, especially that written by of some of the lesser known poets, was seen as merely a weaker version of the Romantics, and thus more backward looking than forward thinking.

It was the emergence of the realistic, biting poetry that came out of the War that finally put the Georgian Movement in the shade. The emerging 'Modernists', as they were to be known as, included poets that had previously allied themselves with the 'Georgians'. They made a truly great impact upon the public, both then and now, and this is where Owen's finest achievement lay.

Rupert Brooke came out of the 'Georgian' period of poetry. He was golden-haired, debonair and handsome; and he was lauded for his verse, although he would later be described as naïve and sentimental. But his poetry was of its time and in1915 was written for a country yet to fully face the War's devastating effects. Who can say that his poetry would not have become less idealistic, less heroic, had he not died at 27 years of age in 1915? His war poetry has received as much criticism as it has praise, but should be considered in context of the year in which it was published:

> *'If I should die, think only this of me:*
> *That there's some corner of a foreign field*
> *That is forever England.'*
>
> *Extract, 'The Soldier', Rupert Brooke, 1914*

Brooke died whilst serving in the Royal Navy, lauded by such greats as Virginia Woolf, Henry James and Winston Churchill, all of whom endorsed his early reputation, guaranteeing him lasting recognition as an early War poet.

Rupert Brooke 1887-1915

Owen struggled on with life at Dunsden until 1913. Evangelism held no sway with him and the lack of support in his passion for poetry and literature contributed to his longing for change. The lifestyle he endured was also seriously affecting his health. Eventually, and by mutual agreement, he went home to his mother but unfortunately, soon after the move, he suffered a protracted illness, ambiguously referred to as 'congestion of the lungs' by the doctor. During a period of recuperation, he gave up to the intense maternal care of Susan, enjoying attention that absolutely focused on his well-being. However, he also knew that this state of affairs could not last when his father was not financially able to shoulder the burden of four growing offspring. Teaching seemed to be his only option and eventually, he left for France to spend time as a language tutor at the Berlitz School of Languages in Bordeaux. This turned out to be a move that would suit him very well and was certainly an improvement upon his time at Dunsden.

Apart from one brief visit back to England, Owen would remain in France for the next two years. He found liberation and opportunity, and the means to express himself far more freely than he had done at any other time in his life. But sadly, and for reasons not entirely under his control, this also would not last.

France provided an easy untroubled life. In his second year, he moved in with the Leger family at Bagneres-de-Bigorre, at the foothills of the Pyrenees, to tutor Mme. Leger and her daughter. The work was untaxing and the company pleasurable when both the wife and daughter of Charles Leger were vying for his attention. His health improved immeasurably. The Leger family was actively interested and involved in the Arts and he would also meet the celebrated poet and public speaker, Laurent Tailhade, a friend of M. Leger, who gave lectures close by.

The works and views of many public figures he had come into contact with – both dead and alive – influenced Owen's growth as a poet. From the forces and wonders of nature, to the brutality of war, he used all he had learned to date and ultimately developed his own voice and style. He wrote with the conviction of a poet who had experience to match his skill as an extremely talented writer. In doing so, almost half a century later, he would radically alter opinion on the way war was viewed.

5

The onset of war

On 3 August 1914, war was declared between France and Germany, but the censorship of information along with the propaganda put about by the French government sheltered Owen and many others from the reality of what was happening. It was only when Tailhade realised the enormity of the situation that his lectures took a new turn and he spoke out about the importance of the voice of the poet during times of war. Owen was hooked and the influence of Tailhade is evident when he wrote to his mother:

> 'Do you know what would hold me together on a battlefield?: The sense that I was perpetuating the language in which Keats and the rest of them wrote!'
>
> *3 December, 1914, Bordeaux, to Susan Owen*

War and fighting were the last things on Owen's mind during the time he spent with the Leger family in France. The initial and appalling French losses were hidden from the general public as much as possible. Although military service was compulsory in France, the government did not want to shake the belief that the war was not as serious as hindsight would prove. At the same time, Owen was far enough away from home to not be subject to the barrage of recruitment posters that encouraged British men to enlist. It was only when reports reached him of the severity of the conflict, as well as the number of young men volunteering, that his conscience was pricked. By the end of summer 1915, two and quarter million men had volunteered in Britain and Owen himself finally enlisted in 1915, preferring to volunteer rather than wait for conscription.

On 21 October, Owen joined the 28th Battalion of the London Regiment (Artists' Rifles). He was listed as being 5 feet 5 inches tall, (coincidentally, the same height as Lawrence of Arabia when he enlisted) having perfect vision with physical development, fair. Joining the Artists' Rifles would seem to combine his artistic temperament with a sense of duty in volunteering. The Regiment was created in 1859 and Owen was thrilled to know that the Victorian artists Leighton and Millais had once belonged to it. Owen was not so thrilled with the life of a soldier in training however, even though it was the closest he would become to mixing with men of a public school background (the lack of which he felt held him back) and who took to the life rather more readily.

Having completed training, and increasing his chest size by one and a half inches to thirty-eight, Owen applied for a commission. He was recommended to serve with the Manchester Regiment, a position he had twice turned down before. He believed that he had nothing in common with the men, writing:

'The generality of men are hard-handed, hard-headed miners, dogged loutish, ugly.'

Letter to Susan, 19 June 1916

December 1916 would see him fighting in France with the Lancashire Fusiliers and having fought with these men in battle, Owen came to have a change of heart and an opposing view. The Regiment was not a glamorous one, but Owen enjoyed the life of an officer with all the privileges it entailed. He began to view the men he had once derided in a different light, appreciating their strength, their loyalty and their commitment in times of war.

War on the Front, 1917

In a letter to Susan on New Year's Day in 1917, Owen realised that he would be sent to fight at the Front in France and, more in hope than expectation, wrote to his mother:

'I don't think it is the real front I'm going to'.

A mere six days later this was amended to:

'...I must not disguise from you the fact that we are at one of the worst parts of the Line'.

Then on 16 January, the awful truth became apparent:

'I have not been at the Front.
    I have been in front of it'.

After taking part in horrific fighting on the Western

29

Front at St. Quentin, he had survived much but in April, his luck ran out. A shell exploded several yards from where he slept killing some of his closest friends and comrades.

Hit by trench mortar, he was first sent to the Welsh Hospital at Netley in Hampshire. Trying to reassure his mother that he was quite well he wrote:

'I sleep well and show every sign of health, except in the manipulation of this pencil'.

Letter to Susan Owen, 18 June 1917

His hands shook dreadfully and subsequent behaviour following his injuries eventually led to the diagnosis of neurasthenia, or 'shell shock' as the condition is now named. Owen was sent to Craiglockhart War Hospital in Edinburgh for specialist treatment and was lucky enough to receive compassionate care. Not all casualties were treated so well.

'Shell shock' was an affliction not greatly understood as it is today. Neurasthenia was the term first used in 1869 by George Beard, an American neurologist. It denoted a condition related to fatigue, anxiety, heart palpitations, high blood pressure, neuralgia and depression - all symptoms very likely to have been brought on through the experiences of War.

Following injury at the Front and recuperation at Craiglockhart, Owen was desperate to see his mother and made it plain that he did not want to share her visits with anyone else. In a letter to Nelly Bulman, a close friend of his mother's who sent him strawberries and cream at the hospital, on 1 July, 1917 he wrote:

'I am not able to settle down here without seeing
Mother. I feel a sort of reserve and suspense about
everything I do.'

Undoubtedly, Susan's presence helped his initial
recovery process enormously (prior to meeting Sassoon
who would be an equal, if not greater benefit to his recovery). Later, in Scarborough, when he knew that he would
be going back to France, he was overcome with homesick-
ness, writing to her:

'I am quite wretched tonight, missing you so much. Oh
so much...I am talking volubly while I write...I am also
thinking wildly and crying a little for only you to hear.'

6

Siegfried Sassoon, a meeting of minds

Siegfried Sassoon was the greatest single influence on Owen's poetical life as well as a very close friend. Owen met Sassoon whilst recovering from his injuries at Craiglockhart where he was a fellow sufferer of 'shell shock'. Knowing of Sassoon's reputation as a poet, he initially dare not introduce himself, believing that he fell far short of Sassoon's already recognised talent. He saw someone he admired enormously and was reluctant to impose himself on this great man, despite all they had in common.

Sassoon had spoken out against the War, against the government and against the generals who sent swathes of young men to almost guaranteed slaughter. Beneath the façade of injury and 'shell shock', Owen came to know the real reason why Sassoon had been sent to Craiglockhart:

'He is here you know because he wrote a letter to the Higher Command which was too plain spoken. They promptly sent him over here!'

Letter to Susan, 15 August 1917

Addressing the House of Commons, Sassoon had written:

'I believe that this war, upon which I entered as a war of defence and liberation, has now become a war of aggression and conquest.' 'I believe it (the letter) may help to destroy the callous complacency with which the majority of those at home regard the continuance of agonies which they do not share and which they have not enough imagination to realise'

(Extracts of a letter read to the House of Commons 6 July 1917)

Owen's meeting with Sassoon cannot be underestimated, both in terms of his poetry and his personal life. This pivotal time would see Owen begin to blossom into the poet he would become, a formidable talent and someone who would capture the spirit and essence of the First World War.

Friendship with Sassoon gave Owen the hope and encouragement he needed; the capacity to change; and the confidence to write about what he saw and how he felt about it. Sassoon was his literary hero, as was Keats, but this one was very much alive and one that he would come to know on a much deeper and personal level within a very short period of time. Sassoon, with his strong anti-war

S F TAYLOR

inclinations, expressed through his poetry, was not afraid to make those feelings known. He was a realist and not given to flights of fancy, but nevertheless still expressing the beauty of nature in his work.

A lifelong friendship (or what was left of life for Owen) ensued between the two men and it was Sassoon who encouraged Owen to further use his experience of war in his poetry. Undoubtedly, he helped guide and see him through a very turbulent time.

Siegfried Sassoon 1886-1967

Owen's poetry at that time was still fairly undistinguished and he had few literary friends, or indeed any contacts at all, in the right circles. Meeting Sassoon was a major turning point in his writing, along with his subsequent introduction to other poets and literary grandees of the time.

In a letter to Sassoon in 1917, Owen expressed his thoughts on what their friendship meant to him:

'Know that since mid-September, when you still regarded me as a tiresome little knocker on your door, I held you as Keats + Christ + Elijah + my Colonel + my father-confessor + Amenophis 1V in profile...And you

34

have fixed my Life – however short. You did not light me: I was always a mad comet; but you have fixed me.'

5th November 1917

By May 1918, Sassoon had returned to active service. He was promoted to lieutenant and after spending a short time in Palestine, returned to the Front at Arras but on 13 July, he was again wounded. This time it was by 'friendly fire' when a British soldier mistook him for a German. He was shot in the head. Sassoon was lucky to survive and as a result of his serious injuries, he spent the rest of the War in Britain. Owen was wretched on hearing the news about Sassoon:

'This time surely he has done with war.

The most encouraging thing is that he is writing again.

Now I must throw my little candle on his torch, and go out again. There are rumours of a large draft of officers shortly.'

Letter to Susan Owen, 30 July 1918

Robert Graves

It was Sassoon who introduced Owen to Robert Graves. During October 1917 a momentous meeting was held between Owen, Sassoon and Graves, at Baberton Golf Club, near Edinburgh, at the time when Sassoon and Owen were still recuperating at Craiglockhart. The conversations can only be imagined, but snippets from letters have revealed the impression each had made on one another. Ultimately, all three were to arguably become the greatest poets of the First World War.

Owen described Graves to his mother as

'a big, rather plain fellow, the last man on earth apparently capable of the extraordinary, delicate fancies in his books'.

From the start, Graves saw great potential in Owen's poetry and was very impressed by what he was given to read Encouraged by Sassoon, Graves wrote to Owen:

'Don't make any mistake, Owen, you are a damned fine poet already & are going to be more so… Puff out your chest a little, Owen & be big – for you've more right than most of us… So outlive this War.'

December 1917

Robert Graves 1895-1985 (Graves Family Archive)

However, a further letter to Owen from Graves also suggested that he felt the realism had gone too far when he wrote:

'For God's sake, cheer up and write more optimistically –
The war's not ended yet, but a poet should have a spirit
above wars.'

Whatever Graves' take on the War, he felt that anti-War poetry was not always helpful. He commented that Sassoon 'thinks he is best employed by writing poems which will make people find the war so hateful that they'll stop it at once at whatever cost. I don't. I think that I'll do more good by keeping up my brother soldiers' morale as far as I can'.

Owen's take on such matters coincided more with Sassoon than Graves and it has been suggested that

Owen's poem 'Apologia Pro Poemate Meo' had been
written in response to Graves' letter of 1917:

'I, too, saw God through mud, -
The mud that cracked on cheeks when wretches
*   smiled.*
War brought more glory to their eyes than blood,
And gave their laughs more glee than shakes a child.

Merry it was to laugh there —
Where death becomes absurd and life absurder.
For power was on us as we slashed bones bare
Not to feel sickness or remorse of murder.

Extract Apologia Pro Poemate Meo,
written at Scarborough,
November/December 1917

As time went on, Owen increasingly saw the need to be
truthful and the essence of his poetry does just that. As
long as he survived the War, he wanted to speak up for
those who had not. The beauty of life in Bordeaux; the
beauty of the poetry of Keats and Shelley; and the beauty
he saw in the natural world around him were blown to
shreds in the trenches of France in 1917. The vivid
descriptions in 'The Sentry' leave little to the imagination
of the conditions endured on both sides. On taking a
German trench he wrote:

Crumbs on the Carpet

'Rain guttering down in waterfalls of slime,
Kept slush waist-high and rising hour by hour,
And choked the steps too thick with clay to climb.
What murk of air remained stank old, and sour
With fumes from whizz-bangs, and the smell
          of men
Who'd lived there years, and left their curse in
          the den,
If not their corpses...'

Extract from The Sentry, begun at
Craiglockhart, 1917, continued at
Scarborough, completed in France

7

The calm before the storm

The Clarence Gardens Hotel in Scarborough was a time
of reflection for Owen, a settled period in his life where he
wrote regularly to his mother and other members of his
family and friends, on his day-to-day activities. Poetry, as
ever uppermost in his mind, took prominence whenever he
had the chance to write in between duties. Owen described
himself as 'majo domo' in charge of domestic arrange-
ments and minor matters of administration. He told his
mother:

'I have to control the Household, which consists of some dozen Batmen, 4 Mess Orderlies, 2 Buglers, the Cook, (a fat woman of great skill) two female kitcheners, and various charwomen! They need driving. You should see me scooting the buglers round our dining-room on their knees with dustpan and brush! You should hear me rate the Charwoman for leaving the Lavatory-Basins unclean. I am responsible for finding rooms for newcomers, which is a great worry, as we are full up. This means however that I have a good room to myself, as well as my office!'

Letter to Susan Owen, 23 November 1917

Life was not uncomfortable at the Hotel considering the deprivations he had endured at the Front in France. Here, officers were fed very well, despite the national shortages, and physically at least, life was such that he settled into Scarborough quite easily. He was kept very busy, which probably suited his state of mind and usefully followed recuperation techniques propounded at Craiglockhart.

In between his duties and writing as much as he was allowed, he read as widely as possible, even compiling a list 'Books Read at Scarborough', during December that year. Prominent on the list is 'Under Fire' by Henri Barbusse. The book is a moving, emotional account of the terrors of life and death on the Western Front, much of it written from the trenches. It is probable that the book further mobilised Owen's own thoughts on the War and the seeming disregard of lives that were sacrificed. As comfortable as he may have been, and as relieved as he must have felt to remain away from the fighting, he was also aware that the time might come when he would have to go back. More in hope than conviction, however, he wrote to his mother, 'I think I am marked Permanent Home Service'.

Around this time, and perhaps after reading Barbusse, Owen produced his first draft of 'The Show'

'My soul looked down from a vague height with Death,
    As remembering how I rose or why,
    And saw a sad land, weak with sweats of dearth,
    Grey, cratered like the moon with hollow woe,
    And pitted with great pocks and scabs of Plagues.'

The Show, first draft Scarborough, November 1917

On one hand, Owen re-lives the agonies and pain of the War and on the other he basks in the release of that other world in the comfort of a Scarborough hotel. Writing to his mother at 4pm on a winter's evening, you can imagine Owen basking in front of the fire, during the hours before dinner, reassuring her that all was well for the time being and how much he had settled into his new life in Scarborough. He was comfortable and warm and safe:

'Life here is a mixture of wind, sand, crumbs on carpets, telephones, signatures, clean sheets, shortage of meat, and too many money-sums. But I like it.'

13 December 1917, Scarborough

He began to go to furniture shops and auctions looking for items to furnish a cottage he hoped to buy after the war.

'I took a joy-walk into Scarboro' yesterday & discovered 3 genuine 'Hepplethwaite' chairs. I think I must have 'em.'

Letter to Susan Owen, 3 Dec 1917

However, despite the relaxed and comfortable life that temporarily put aside the terror of fighting in France, Owen, by his own admission, made few friends in Scarborough. Instead, his imagination took him to a future life at the end of the War and he took pleasure in planning for that time:

'I went to an auction yesterday, & got an antique side table wondrous cheap…to be my Cottage sideboard.'

Letter to Susan Owen 9 Dec 1917

Poetry never ceased to be far from his mind and reflections on the War were put into words that would live on far beyond the years in which they were written. Poetry that had begun in Edinburgh reached a stage of completion in Scarborough:

'This afternoon I had a fire in my grate, which smokes horribly in the wind. Thus I finished an important poem this afternoon, in the right atmosphere. I also drafted three others.'

Letter to Susan Owen 3 Dec 1917

The spectre of war would never leave him and the last two lines of 'The Sentry', begun at Craiglockhart between

August and October 1917, continued at Scarborough in May 1918, and finally completed in France in September 1918, perhaps encapsulate the sadness of his own life when it was so cruelly cut short:

> 'Through the dense din, I say, we heard him shout
> 'I see your lights!' – But ours had long gone out.'

Owen had one of the best rooms in the Clarence Gardens Hotel, a five-windowed bay in a corner tower with a view of the sea, In the middle of a wild, wintry day on the East Coast of Yorkshire, on 5 December, he wrote 'Wild With All Regrets', a poem he dedicated to Sassoon. At the foot of the draft he had written 'May I?'. Mortality was uppermost in his mind and the imminence of death was brought into sharp focus when he considered that they might not live long enough to see through to another generation:

> *'We said we'd hate to grow dead-old. But now,*
> *Not to live old seems awful: not to renew*
> *My boyhood with my boys…'*

> *Wild With All regrets, Dec 1917*

He had already asked Sassoon's opinion on the poem, but Sassoon had long been convinced of the brilliance and potential of Owen's work. There was little doubt of Sassoon's admiration.

During that same month, on December 15th, 1917 an armistice had been signed between Russia and Germany, but as early as 10th February 1918 negotiations had already broken down. The War would not end as soon as had been hoped. In a Scarborough oyster bar, Owen wrote that his friend, Philip Bainbrigge, 'opined that the whole of civilization is extremely liable to collapse.'

For now, Owen's time in Scarborough was to be taken advantage of, it was the calm before the final storm of the Western Front, but comfortable as he may have been physically, he was experiencing a restlessness regarding his life in general. Uncertain what was in store for him, New Year's Eve, saw Owen reviewing his past, as many do in wartime or in peace:

> 'I am not satisfied with my years. Everything has been done in bouts: Bouts of awful labour at Shrewsbury and Bordeaux; bouts of amazing pleasure in the Pyrenees, and play at Craiglockhart; bouts of horrible danger on the Somme; bouts of poetry always; of your affection always; of sympathy for the oppressed always.'

On a more optimistic note, his poetry was going well and he took some satisfaction in his place amongst well-regarded fellow poets. He knew in what esteem his contemporaries held him:

> 'I go out of this year a Poet, my dear Mother, as which I did not enter it. I am held peer by the Georgians; I am a poet's poet. I am started. The tugs have left me; I feel the great swelling of the open sea taking my galleon...'

Letter to Susan Owen, 31 December 1917

Not all poets took the same stance. Where Owen was open in his descriptions of the reality of the day to day life, even in letters to his mother, it was not the picture painted back home. Owen did not hold back telling of the grind and misery at the Front; the marching of fatigue parties struggling to dig yet more trenches; the misery of work amongst death and deprivation. Owen's poetry stood up against commonly distorted representations made by the Press. Along with the government, they aimed at reassuring an anxious public who were concerned about their loved ones, and with appeasing the generals who were keen that the whole truth should not be revealed.

'It is a good thing no photographs can be taken by night. If they could they would not appear in the Daily Mirror which I see still depicts the radiant smiles of Tommies 'well behind'.'

The reference here is most likely to the works of Jessie Pope, an English poet, writer and journalist, who remains best known for her patriotic and motivational poems published during the War. Born in 1868, Pope was 46 at the outbreak of the War. She was almost of a different generation to the men who went out to fight, and had previously been recognised for humorous verse and prose written for the popular Press and Punch magazine.

Jessie Pope 1868-1941 (Lafayette, 1929 Private Collection)

After her death, however, her reputation rested more on the patriotic verses and the words 'Jingoistic doggerel' are those most used to describe her output:

> *Our German-made Goliath*
> *taunted Tommy on his size,*
> *But the drubbing Tommy gave*
> *him has caused him*
> *much surprise;*
> *And a hasty memorandum in*
> *the Teuton mind*
> *is stored*
> *'The little British Army must*
> *never be ignored'.*

Pope encouraged men to enlist and was reputed to give

out white feathers to those who refused. Her take on the War reflected more the idealistic aspiration of an unknowing public, and a military who needed to swell their ranks and replace the fallen. It appeared in great contrast to the anti-war poetry of Owen and Sassoon, poets who had actually seen and experienced warfare. Owen found her work in poor taste and originally dedicated his poem 'Dulce et Decorum Est' to "Jessie Pope etc". (Later, this was changed to "a certain Poetess")

The title of his poem comes from the words of Horace, the final line translating as 'it is sweet and right to die for your country'. Although not published until 1920, a draft had been posted to his mother as early as 16 October 1917 along with the words:

'Here is a gas poem, done yesterday, (which is not private, but not final).

The effect of the War was deeply disturbing, and Owen's poetry underwent a great change in style and content as he reflected more and more upon the atrocities he had seen and the atrocities he knew were still happening at the Front. The imagery is horrific and the condemnation of the War emphatic. It is likely this poem, one of his most recognised, most often quoted and most studied, was revised at Scarborough:

Dulce et Decorum Est

Bent double, like old beggars under sacks,
Knock-kneed, coughing like hags, we cursed through
  sludge,
Till on the haunting flares we turned our backs

And towards our distant rest began to trudge.
Men marched asleep. Many had lost their boots
But limped on, blood shod. All went lame; all blind;
Drunk with fatigue; deaf even to the hoots
Of tired, outstripped Five-Nines that dropped
        behind.
Gas! Gas! Quick, boys! – An ecstasy of fumbling,
Fitting the clumsy helmets just in time;
But someone still was yelling out and stumbling,
And flound'ring like a man in fire or lime…
Dim, through the misty panes and thick green light,
As under a green sea, I saw him drowning.

In all my dreams, before my helpless sight,
He plunges at me, guttering, choking, drowning.
If in some smothering dreams you too could pace
Behind the wagon that we flung him in,
And watch the white eyes writhing in his face,
His hanging face, like a devil's sick of sin;
If you could hear, at every jolt, the blood
Come gargling from the froth-corrupted lungs,
Obscene as cancer, bitter as the cud
Of vile, incurable sores on innocent tongues, -
My friend, you would not tell with such high zest
To children ardent for some desperate glory,
The old lie: Dulce et decorum est
Pro patria mori.'

Revised Scarborough Jan/Mar 1918

'Spring Offensive', probably begun in Scarborough the following summer, then revised in France, is equally damning. In it, Owen gives a vivid account of the action and aftermath of an attack that probably took place in April 1917:

> *So, soon they topped the hill, and raced together*
> *Over an open stretch of herb and heather*
> *Exposed. And instantly the whole sky burned*
> *With fury against them; earth set sudden cups*
> *In thousands for their blood; and the green slope*
> *Chasmed and deepened sheer to infinite space.*
>
> *Of them who running on that last high place*
> *Breasted the surf of bullets, or went up*
> *On the hot blast and fury of hell's upsurge,*
> *Or plunged and fell away past this wold's verge,*
> *Some say God caught them even before they fell.*

Extract, Spring Ofensive, July 1918

Owen's take on the War highlighted the camaraderie, the morbid humour and the closeness shared by the men, as well as the inherent horror. He saw no glory, nor appreciation of any higher spirit:

> *'Merry it was to laugh there –*
> *Where death becomes absurd and life absurder.*
> *For power was on us as we slashed bones bare*
> *Not to feel sickness or remorse or murder.'*

Extract, Apologia pro poemate meo,
December 1917

Religion held very little place in his heart and in February 1918, Owen sent his mother the first draft of

'Last 'Words'. He believed that prayer was 'indistinguishable from blasphemy when he wrote:

> *'O Jesus Christ!' one fellow sighed.*
> *And kneeled, and bowed, tho' not in prayer, and*
> *   died.*
> *And the Bullets sang – 'In vain'*
> *Machine Guns chuckled 'Vain'*
> *Big Guns guffawed 'In vain'*

Extract of early draft of 'The Last Laugh',
February 1918

Owen was happy to receive confirmation that another poem, 'Miners' had been accepted for publication in 'The Nation', one of the few publications that were critical of the War. The poem was also only one of five to be published during Owen's lifetime.

At the beginning of 1918, life was still relatively upbeat and Owen still had one eye on a future life for himself outside that of being a soldier:

'It occurs to me that I should make a really workmanlike Dealer in Antiques. If I could get a shop in London and some experienced Hands I should not be uncontent'

Letter to Susan Owen, 14 Feb 1918

This came on the back of a visit to a 'secret Old Shop' where he discovered a 'perfect chair' and a 'filthy old Chest of Drawers of lovely proportions and precious oak.' He also admitted 'I think I have found what I want at last'.

The life of an antiques dealer sadly remained a dream

and the War beckoned once again. In April 1918, Owen was granted a 48-hour leave to spend in Shrewsbury with his parents. His brother, Harold, was also there. Harold asked if Wilfred had planned to go back to the front line and received the reply:

> 'Yes, I have, Harold, and I know I shall be killed. But it's the only place that I can make my protest from.'

It was a poignant remark that became prophetically true.

The Sitwells

In May that same year, Owen had been given three weeks leave before reporting back for duty at Scarborough and during this time he made most of the opportunity to make acquaintance with the Sitwell family, in particular Osbert.

Siblings Edith, Sacheverell and Osbert Sitwell had spent much of their early life at Woodend in Scarborough, the Sitwell family seat from 1870 to 1934. They became renowned in the 1920s and 1930s for their poetry and writings, which stood alongside many acclaimed writers of their time.

The Sitwells represented the modernist approach to poetry and literature, in comparison to Owen, who up to the time of his introduction to Osbert was viewed as old fashioned.

Owen went to London where, at the behest of Sassoon, he met Osbert for the first time. Osbert was a good friend of Sassoon and knew that they would get on; he also wanted to push Owen's poetry out into the public domain.

At this time, Osbert Sitwell had already spoken out, and written against, the War and proved to be very receptive.

Woodend in Scarborough, home of the Sitwells
– now a creative arts space

ROBERT ROSS, another friend of Sassoon's, as well as Oscar Wilde, was a recognised figure in London literary circles and facilitated the meeting at his flat. Osbert was told that Owen would be rather shy, but on first meeting he warmed to him at once. He recalled later the 'immense esteem in which he [Owen] held literature…To him they [books] were all-important, while poetry was the very crown of life, and constituted its meaning.'

Osbert later spoke of Owen as having 'a well-proportioned voice that signified a sense of justice and compassion'. He described his eyes as 'deep in colour, and dark in their meaning'.

He was very taken with Owen but also noted that his 'whole appearance, in spite of what he had been through, gave the impression of being somewhat young for his age, and, though he seemed perfectly sure of himself, it was easy to perceive that by nature he was shy'.

They shared in common…

'a delight in the company of our friends, a love of books, and a hatred of modern war and of those who did not feel its burden'.

Osbert Sitwell, Noble Essences 1950

Following this meeting, Owen knew that he was finally achieving recognition by his peers and was thrilled to be invited to meet Osbert's siblings, Edith and Sacheverell. Other invitations followed, but there were too many for Owen to accept in such a short period of time. He was excited by the prospect of these introductions but sadly, would never get another opportunity to meet Edith especially when she played such major role in his contributing to the influential 'Wheels' anthology.

'Wheels' an annual miscellany of contemporary poetry founded by Edith, held contributions by poets who were generally regarded as anti-War. Owen had already read an earlier edition of 'Wheels' and perhaps further developed his style based on its content. However, he did not send anything at that time, possibly because he wanted to first work on the poetry he had only in draft form. Owen was not after fame 'at all cost' and wrote to his mother in 1918:

'And I want no limelight, and celebrity is the last infirmity I desire. Fame is the recognition of one's peers. I have already more than their recognition'

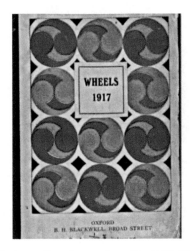

Anthology of poetry produced by Edith Sitwell

When Owen had first tried to buy a copy of the 1917 edition of Wheels, from Canning's Scarborough bookshop (no longer in existence), it was not easy to come by:

'Rigby's people would not order a single copy without deposit!

Letter to Osbert Sitwell, July 1918

After visiting the Sitwells, Owen returned to Scarborough during the first week in June and was billeted in a tent with a cinder floor in the Cavalry Barracks – not back in the comfort of the Clarence Gardens Hotel. However, he soon changed the location of his tent for one more suited to his temperament, a place with long grass and buttercups all around.

Sacheverell, Edith and Osbert Sitwell

It was shortly after setting up camp that Owen wrote of receiving an urgent request from the Sitwells in London...

'...for more of my poetry for their 1918 anthology which is coming out immediately. This on the strength of 'The Deranged', which S. Moncrieff showed them the other day. I know not what to do. For one thing I want to see the Sitwells' etc. works before I decide to co-appear in a book!'

Sacheverell, Edith and Osbert Sitwell

The Deranged' was believed to have been drafted in Ripon in May 1918, and revised in Scarborough in July of the same year:

> *'Who are these? Why sit they here in twilight?*
> *Wherefore rock they, purgatorial shadows,*
> *Drooping tongues from jaws that slob their relish,*
> *Baring teeth that leer like skulls' teeth wicked?'*

Owen had started to put together a collection of poems

for his book: 'Disabled and Other Poems'. In the preface, left only as a rough draft, he wrote:

> 'This book is not about heroes. English poetry is not yet fit to speak of them. Nor is it about deeds, or lands, nor anything about glory, honour, might, majesty, dominion, or power, except War. Above all, I am not concerned with Poetry.
>
> My subject is War, and the pity of War.
>
> The poetry is in the pity.
>
> …All a poet can do to-day is warn. That is why the true poets must be truthful.'

His words serve as a reminder of all that Owen held true. He created a vision of war in his poetry that went beyond descriptions of the pain and horror around him. He sought to dispel once and for all the idea of war as something 'noble' by exposing the reality of what it meant to fight at the Front.

During his final days at Scarborough, before returning to France, it was known that Owen was working towards submitting eight pieces. Sadly, he had missed the deadline but the 'Wheels' anthology of 1919 was dedicated to his memory. It included 'Strange Meeting' (claimed by Osbert Sitwell to be Owen's chief and most moving work) 'The Show', 'A Terre', 'The Sentry', 'Disabled', 'The Deadbeat' and 'The Chances'. The original manuscripts were originally kept in the Sitwell family collection as a lasting legacy, but were later acquired by the British Library in 1934.

> *And of my weeping something had been left,*
> *Which must die now. I mean the truth untold,*
> *The pity of war, the pity war distilled.*
> *Now men will go content with what we spoiled,*

Or, discontent, boil bloody, and be spilled'

Extract Strange Meeting, drafted
Scarborough 1918

...There we herded from the blast
Of whizz-bangs; but one found our door at last, -
Buffeting eyes and breath, snuffing the candles,
And thud! flump! thud! down the steep steps came
    thumping
And sploshing in the flood, deluging muck,
The sentry's body; then his rifle, handles
Of old Boche bombs, and mud in ruck on ruck.
We dredged it up, for dead, until he whined,
'O sir – my eyes – I'm blind, - I'm blind, - I'm
    blind.'

Extract The Sentry, developed in
Scarborough, May 1918

His poetry had at long last reached a pinnacle of brilliance, encapsulating his vision and truth of war. During May 1918, the month he met with Osbert Sitwell in London, he completed twenty poems at Scarborough.

Sassoon wrote an introduction to a later anthology of Owen's work, using manuscripts passed on by Susan Owen, and Edith chose seven poems for inclusion. The book was dedicated to Owen's memory and published in 1920. It was through Wheels and the anthology that Owen came to be recognised as a 'Modernist' poet rather than the 'Georgian' he had earlier believed himself to be. It was also after publication, and after his death, that Owen's fame was in its ascendance. During August that year,

Owen met Sassoon and Osbert Sitwell for the last time. Sitwell arranged for them all to hear Violet Gordon Wood-house perform on the harpsichord in a private concert where Osbert noted that Owen 'sat dazed with happiness at the fire and audacity of the player'. The concert was followed by tea at Osbert's house in Swan Walk and then a visit to the Physic Garden where they sat in the sun. Osbert Sitwell wrote that 'so listlessly happy was Owen that he could not bring himself to leave the Garden to go to the station and catch the train he had arranged to take.'

Within a week, on August 11th 1918, Owen was ordered to attend for medical inspection where he was certified 'fit to proceed overseas'. He already knew that this was likely to happen, no matter how hard his friends tried to prevent it. Moncrieff had been desperately trying to get him a job through the War Office.

> 'I am glad. That is I am much gladder to be going out again than afraid. I shall be better able to cry my outcry, playing my part...'

> *Letter to Susan Owen, 10 August 1918,*
> *Scarborough*

On 30 August, during Owen's last day with his mother in Hastings, they looked out across the Channel to France where he quoted from Rabindranath Tagore:

> *'When I leave, let these be my parting words: what my eyes have seen, what my life received, are unsurpassable.'*

Two years following the death of her son, Susan Owen

wrote to Tagore when he visited London to tell him how she had found the words written in Wilfred's notebook and that it reminded her of the last words he had spoken to her.

8

Return to the front

In spring 1918, Owen was sent to the training camp in Ripon to get fit for active service once again. He liked Ripon very much and his letters home indicate that he was not too unhappy with his lot, writing that Ripon was 'the pleasantest camp I know'. He writes as often as he can, reads much, and attends plays. He is still making plans for the future and is encouraged by the knowledge that his poetry is in demand. Following a brief visit to London, he learned that Heinemann were interested in publishing his poetry, announcing to Susan that 'My reception' in London has been magnificent.'

Back at Scarborough in June, the months leading up to his return to the Front are passed in preparation with not a little enjoyment in between. The arrival of his requested bicycle gave him pleasure to 'go shopping almost every morning!' when he was still on the lookout for items for that future cottage. The worst of his days was when he learned of Sassoon's injury that almost killed him. Before embarking on his return to France, he wrote to his friend:

'Goodbye –

dear Siegfried –

I'm much nearer to you here than in Scarborough, and am by so much happier.'

Ending with the words:

'What more is there to say that you will not better understand unsaid.'

31 August 1918

By October he is back in the field witnessing further atrocities that defy explanation and reason:

'I came out to help these boys – directly by leading them as well as an officer can; indirectly by watching their sufferings that I may speak of them as well as a pleader can....

Of whose blood lies yet crimson on my shoulder where his head was – and where so lately yours was – I must not now write.'

Letter to Susan, In the Field, 4/5 October 1918

During his final days in the trenches, Owen reported that 'time on the Somme in 1917 was so infinitely worse than this for cold, privation, and fatigue that nothing daunts me now'. Letters to his mother and to Sassoon saw him stoic and accepting. He was still in charge of 'D' Company but his letter to Sassoon reveals a self-preserving numbness against the fresh fighting he witnesses:

'I cannot say I suffered anything; having let my brain grow dull...the boy by my side, shot through the head, lay on top of me, soaking my shoulder, for half an hour...I shall feel again as soon as I dare, but now I must not. I don't take the cigarette out of my mouth when I write Deceased over their letters.'

Letter to Sassoon 10 October 1918

Owen even manages to sound upbeat the next day in his letter to Susan:

'It is delightful to have the Scarborough Drums to fill the Vacant Ranks. Censoring letters today I came across this: 'Do you know that little officer called Owen who was at Scarborough; he is commanding my Company, and he is a toff I can tell you. No na-poo. Compree?' Interpreted 'a fine fellow, no nonsense about him!'

Letter to Susan Owen 11 October 1918

Less than three weeks later, Owen was stationed in 'The Smoky Cellar of the Forester's House' (as he described it.) A soldier standing by him was peeling potatoes, another chopping wood and a fellow officer snoring on a bench. There were rumours of peace, although orders immediately put paid to any of their hopes with instruction that, 'Peace talk in any form is to cease'. And immediate steps were to be taken to 'ensure this order is obeyed both in the spirit and in the letter'. War was not yet over for Owen's Company even though they knew it was close:

'There is no danger down here, or if any, it will be well over before you read these lines...

'Of this I am certain, you could not be visited by a band of friends half so fine as surround me here.'

31 October 1918

In sharp contrast to the opinion that neurasthenia, or 'shell shock' had been an excuse for cowardice, when Owen returned to the fighting in France he proved to be a brave and superb soldier. It was recorded that in one attack he captured a German machine gun post, taking a great many prisoners, almost single-handedly and for this he was awarded the Military Cross.

On Monday 4 November, Owen took part in fighting for the last time. At 25 years of age, he was killed in the assault on the Sambre-Oise Canal at Ors. It was just one week before armistice was announced. The news of his death reached his parents on 11 November, Armistice Day.

Lieutenant W.E.S. Owen M.C is buried at the village of Ors, where his grave lies between Private W.E. Duckworth and Private H. Topping.

The day after his death, it was reported that he was to be recorded as a full lieutenant with effect from 4 December 1917.

*Owen's gravestone at Ors Communal Cemetery,
France*

Susan tried her best to present a picture of her son as the ultimate hero in looks as well as deeds: more pious than he actually was and taller in stature. In reality, he had long since ceased to share the same faith as his mother and in height he was barely more than five foot five, only just within the height required at the start of the War. Needless to say, neither detracted from all he achieved after enlisting.

Fittingly, Susan chose a quote taken from Owen's poem 'The End' to put on his gravestone, but the quote is incomplete and misleading through incorrect punctuation. The gravestone reads:

'Shall life renew these bodies?
Of a truth all death will he annul'

She omits the question mark at the end of an incomplete sentence and manages to completely change the meaning of the words in which her son had questioned the Christian faith. The poem actually reads:

> 'Shall life renew these bodies? Of a truth
>   All death will he annul, all tears assuage?''

The quote on the headstone gives the impression that faith will prevail. She wanted to think of her son in heaven with the angels, and her religion gave her comfort.

In 1931, Edmund Blunden published Owen's poetry, using the original manuscripts in the process. He wrote to Sassoon of his annoyance that Susan Owen wanted to celebrate her son as a 'tall heroic figure':

> 'Mrs. Owen has had her way, with a purple binding and
> a photograph Wh makes W look like a 6 foot Major who
> had been in East Africa or so for several years.'

However, it would be churlish to dwell on Susan's view of her son, and what mother would not make the most of his achievements at such a time? He was her world and nothing could take away the longer lasting legacy of his own words and poetry. Wilfred Owen is still revered as the ultimate poet of the First World War, read and studied over the past hundred years and more, and his name will live on.

9

A lasting legacy

It was common that those who returned from the War never spoke about their experience, which makes Owen's words so important. His was a voice that articulated all that many could not. Ted Hughes, born in 1930, wrote a number of poems on the impact of the First World War but was acutely aware that his father rarely spoke of it:

> 'I never questioned him directly. Never. I can hardly believe it now, but I didn't. He managed to convey the horror so nakedly that it fairly tortured me when he did speak about it.'
>
> *Taken from a letter to Geoffrey Moorhouse, 8 January 1994.*

Hughes' experience can only cover the indirect impact the War had on his life: on his childhood and his family; and on the community in which those who remained, lived.

From the 1960s to the present day, Wilfred Owen is still taught in the classroom with reference to the man, his poetry and the War. In the study of 'Power and Conflict', the poem 'Exposure' is often used to compare and contrast attitudes on war, its purpose and the perceived realities of what it meant. It is studied alongside Ted Hughes' Bayonet Charge, and Tennyson's Charge of the Light Brigade. Students compare celebrated heroism with stark reality and come to their own conclusions on why the poems were written and how they were received.

Students may also undertake research into 'shell-shock' and the condition now known as 'post traumatic stress disorder' (PTSD), how these conditions were treated both then and now. The ubiquitous 'lessons should be learned' comes to mind, but in reality, very little is. War is still very much with us and around us, even more so with the expansion of social media and communications in all its forms.

Sadly, time is limited and the importance of exams will come to the fore, but the discussion around war and the importance of Owen's poetry will continue to provide much to debate.

Ian McMillan

The 1960s saw the emergence a generation that wanted to wage 'peace not war'. Following on from this, in 2017, the poet Ian McMillan questioned why Owen's stance on war should be the only voice that is heard when there are so many others too. 'Dulce et Decorum Est' has been studied in schools for over fifty years and is held up as definitive when it comes to wartime suffering, but McMillan points out that the poem, although taken from experience, is still a 'work of fiction'. He says that 'in the 1960s a literary elite decided this was the most authentic view of the conflict because it chimed with their own anti-war feelings.'

BBC, World War One presented by Ian McMillan,

Owen's poetry had inspired McMillan, and still does, but he introduces other 'realities' of war that are also worthy of consideration; the ordinary soldier wondering where the next rum ration was coming from; the writings in the 'Wipers Times', a satirical newspaper published in the trenches that poked fun at the Germans and their own officers alike, using humour to raise morale. He also highlights the role of women, pointing out that a quarter of poems published during the War were by women (and not just Jessie Pope styled verses). Poet Charlotte Mew wrote:

*'Not yet will those measureless
fields be green again
Where only yesterday the wild
sweet blood of wonderful youth was shed;
There is a grave whose earth must
hold too long, too deep a stain,
Though for ever over it we may
speak as proudly as we may tread'.*

The Cenotaph, Charlotte May, 1919

An anthology of her work was published by Harold Monro's Bookshop in 1916 and was praised by Siegfried Sassoon although, sadly, she is not widely recognised for her work.

T.E. Lawrence

LAWRENCE HAD ALSO SEEN active service in the First World War and was a contemporary of Owen. He had fought with the Arabs to free the stranglehold of the Ottoman Empire, and was instrumental in their success. However, he made no secret of his distaste for war and the excesses of killing, whether it was the by the enemy or by those he fought alongside. During his later conversations with Sassoon, he showed empathy with Owen and said at the time:

> 'Sassoon told me a lot about him. Owen was a decent fellow, very modest and not tolerant.'

His summing up of Owen in those few words is succinct, yet apt: decent, modest and not tolerant.

On first meeting, Sassoon, knowing that Lawrence was a colonel, expected a typical military man to be introduced, but was relieved to find him pleasant and unassuming, and that he could talk intelligently about literature. The Lawrence he met was nothing like the action-man hero portrayed by the media.

Lawrence and Sassoon admired one another's achievements and surely there can be little doubt that had Owen survived the War, he would equally have been part of that friendship.

Sassoon expressed protectiveness towards Lawrence as he had done to Owen, noting the vulnerability that sat alongside the strength and determination of each man.

T.E. Lawrence , (1888-1935) (British Army File)

LAWRENCE TOLD Sassoon that he had a huge admiration for those in the literary and poetic world, including Hardy, Forster and Owen, and indeed Sassoon himself.

Osbert Sitwell

Although Sitwell had the privilege of knowing Owen during his lifetime, his reminiscences in volume three of his autobiography of 1950 bring together that knowledge with his subsequent reflection. He begins his chapter on Owen with the words:

'Wilfred Owen! This is a name that has gathered a continual accretion of fire. It glows. It lives clothed in flame...'

Osbert Sitwell (1892-1969) (National Portrait
Gallery)

Dylan Thomas

Like Owen, Thomas was not quick to embrace war or
to enlist, but as a young man during World War Two he
did eventually help the war effort with his propaganda
films. As the War progressed, his poetry focused on death,
an obsession throughout his adult life, and this was
embodied in his writing of the War. The moving and
memorable 'Ceremony After a Fire Raid' spoke of the
death of a newborn child after an air raid:

> *'Among the street burned to tireless death*
> *A child of a few hours*
> *With its kneading mouth*
> *Charred on the black breast of the grave'*
>
> Ceremony After a Fire Raid, 1945

When Dylan read Owen's poetry he found sentiments that reflected those of his own and wrote of him:

> ... it is the preface by Wilfred Owen, to a volume of his poems which was to show, to England, and the intolerant world, the foolishness, unnaturalness, horror, inhumanity, and insupportability of war, and to expose, so that all could suffer and see, the heroic lies, the willingness of the old to sacrifice the young, indifference, grief, the soul of soldiers ... he is a poet of all times, all places, and all wars. There is only one war: that of men against men."

Dylan Thomas, (1914-1953) 1952 New York, Gotham Book Shop

Jeremy Paxman

Paxman, British broadcaster, journalist, author, and latterly quizmaster of University Challenge is no stranger to conflict and worked for the BBC as a reporter from 1974 – 1977. He is also author of 'A Higher Form Of Killing' (1982), a history of chemical and biological warfare written with the journalist Robert Harris. He is known for his strong views and a particular style of interviewing. In 1998, he won a Royal Television Society Award for his tenacious interview with the British Home Secretary Michael Howard in which he asked the same question 17 times.

In 2007, Paxman wrote an article on Owen, first published in The Telegraph in November that year, to coincide with a BBC4 programme 'Wilfred Owen: A Remembrance Tale.' At his request, his fee was donated to the Poppy Appeal. His presentation left viewers in no doubt of the personal respect and appreciation he holds for Owen's poetry:

'For me, he is the greatest of all the war poets. But there is nothing original in my enthusiasm...The fascination of his life is his embodiment of contradictions...he was not among the first to answer the call to bash the Boche...[perhaps a reference here to the poetry of Jessie Pope] but his letters to his mother...show how much he changed. Initial distaste at the vulgarity of the sweaty, noisy men among whom he was obliged to live became a genuine love.'

Jeremy Paxman, (1950-) Sunday Times 2017

Philip Larkin

Larkin is not readily associated with views on war. Having been pronounced unfit for service during World War Two, due to poor eyesight, he had no direct involvement with wartime conflict. However, he did possess an ability to articulate the emotions of ordinary people who did not have a voice.

Fifty years following the end of the Great War, he wrote a poem, probably inspired by a photograph taken at the time, describing ordinary men who were queuing to enlist in 1914:

> *'Those long uneven lines*
> *Standing as patiently*
> *As if they were stretched outside*
> *The Oval or Villa Park,*
> *The crowns of hats, the sun*
> *On moustached archaic faces*
> *Grinning as if it were all*
> *An August Bank Holiday lark'*

And ending with the lines:

> *Never such innocence,*
> *Never before or since,*
> *As changed itself to past*
> *Without a word – the men*
> *Leaving the gardens tidy,*
> *The thousands of marriages*
> *Lasting a little while longer:*
> *Never such innocence again*

Philip Larkin, MCMXIV, 1964

Eleven years later, in 1975, Larkin wrote an essay on Owen which was later included in Larkin's 'Required Writing: miscellaneous pieces 1955-1982'. Here, Larkin was as much concerned with Owen the man as he was with Owen the poet and considered the drip feed of biographical information that had been made available in the years since the poet's death.

Larkin wrote:

> 'A writer's reputation is twofold: that what we think of his work, and what we think of him. What's more, we expect the two halves to relate: if they don't, then one or other of our opinions alters until they do.'

Larkin highlights the relationship between Owen and his mother and the fact that 631 of his surviving 673 letters are addressed to her alone.

The influence of his mother, for good or bad, is not lost on him:

> 'For what the letters cry out on every page is that it was she who magnetized his love, his intimacy, his tenderness'.

Larkin may also have reflected on his own relationship with his mother and its impact upon his life and his writing.

Philip Larkin 1922-1985 (Fay Godwin 1970)

Larkin noted that Owen had written to her confessing:

'At bottom, it is that I ought to be in love and am not'.

Owen was fully aware that he had few feelings of tenderness for anyone, and certainly expressed very few apart from those he showed to his mother. It cannot be fully established what influence this had on his poetry, and whether or not it would have continued in later years had he lived, but the influence of war must surely have been far greater.

Above all, Larkin appreciated the enormity of the effect of the War, of how Owen the man had changed, and with it, Owen the poet:

'From being an unimpressive and derivative poet, he became an original and unforgettable one. From lacking 'any touch of tenderness' [Owen's words] he became the spokesman of a deep and unaffected compassion. From being an unlikeable youth he became a likeable and admirable man'

In conclusion

In 1914, Owen's poetry was mediocre at best. His talent lay untapped, but was continually developing. It was as if writing at this time was just a practice for what was to come; scratching the surface. Whilst retaining the gentle side of his nature, by 1918 he would unleash an anger that rose from knowledge and experience. It cut into to the reality of war with an unerring accuracy that left the reader in no doubt about the suffering and mass slaughter of the men on both sides of the conflict.

Poetry begun at Craiglockhart and encouraged by Sassoon, was completed in Scarborough and the powerful finished works presented a clear and certain voice that represented those who otherwise would never be heard. Wilfred Owen came to be amongst the most respected and revered poets of his generation even though he only lived to twenty-five years of age.

In 2017, sculptor Anthony Padgett created a bust of Owen and presented it to the town of Shrewsbury where Owen spent much of his early life. Of the likeness, Padgett said:

'The bust is in a figurative style, characteristic of many artworks from the period in which he lived, and echoes the bust of the poet Keats, whom Owen admired'.

It is built on to a World War One shell case and is

based on extensive research of biographies and photographs of Owen and has correct military badges and buttons.

Bust of Owen by Anthony Padgett, 2017

10

Last words

It is fitting that the final words of this book should be left to those of Siegfried Sassoon, words that encapsulate the very essence of Wilfred Owen.

Sassoon wrote two of the finest testimonials to Owen, written both as friend and poet, and are contained in the collection of poetry published after Owen's death:

'He was a man of absolute integrity of mind. He never wrote his poems (as so many war-poets did) to make the effect of a personal gesture. He pitied others; he did not pity himself. In the last year of his life he attained a clear vision of what he needed to say, and these poems survive him as his true and splendid testament'.

'In writing an introduction such as this it is good to be brief. The poems printed in this book need no preliminary commendations from me or anyone else. The author has left us his own fragmentary but impressive Foreword; this, and his Poems, can speak for him, backed by the authority of his experience as an infantry soldier, and sustained by nobility and originality of style. All that was strongest in Wilfred Owen survives in his poems; any superficial impression impressions of his personality, any records of his conversation, behaviour, or appearance, would be irrelevant and unseemly. The curiosity which demands such morsels would be incapable of appreciating the richness of his work.'

Siegfried Sassoon

Wilfred Owen 1893 -1918

'I forgot hunger in the hunger for life'
Written to Susan Owen from the Front in France, 1917

Biblography

Wilfred Owen Collected Letters. Ed. Harold Owen and
John Bell
Oxf UP 1967 London

Wilfred Owen The War Poems ed. Jon Stallworthy
London Chatto and Windus 1994

Wilfred Owen A biography Jon Stallworthy
London Oxf UP 1974

Dominic Hibberd Wilfred Owen the last year. London,
Constable, 1994

Dominic Hibberd, Wilfred Owen. London, Phoenix, 2003

Cuthbertson, Guy. Wilfred Owen. New Haven, Yale
University Press, 2014

Larkin, Philip. Required writing, London, Faber and
Faber, 1983

Bibliography

Sitwell, Osbert. Noble Essences, London, Macmillan, 1950